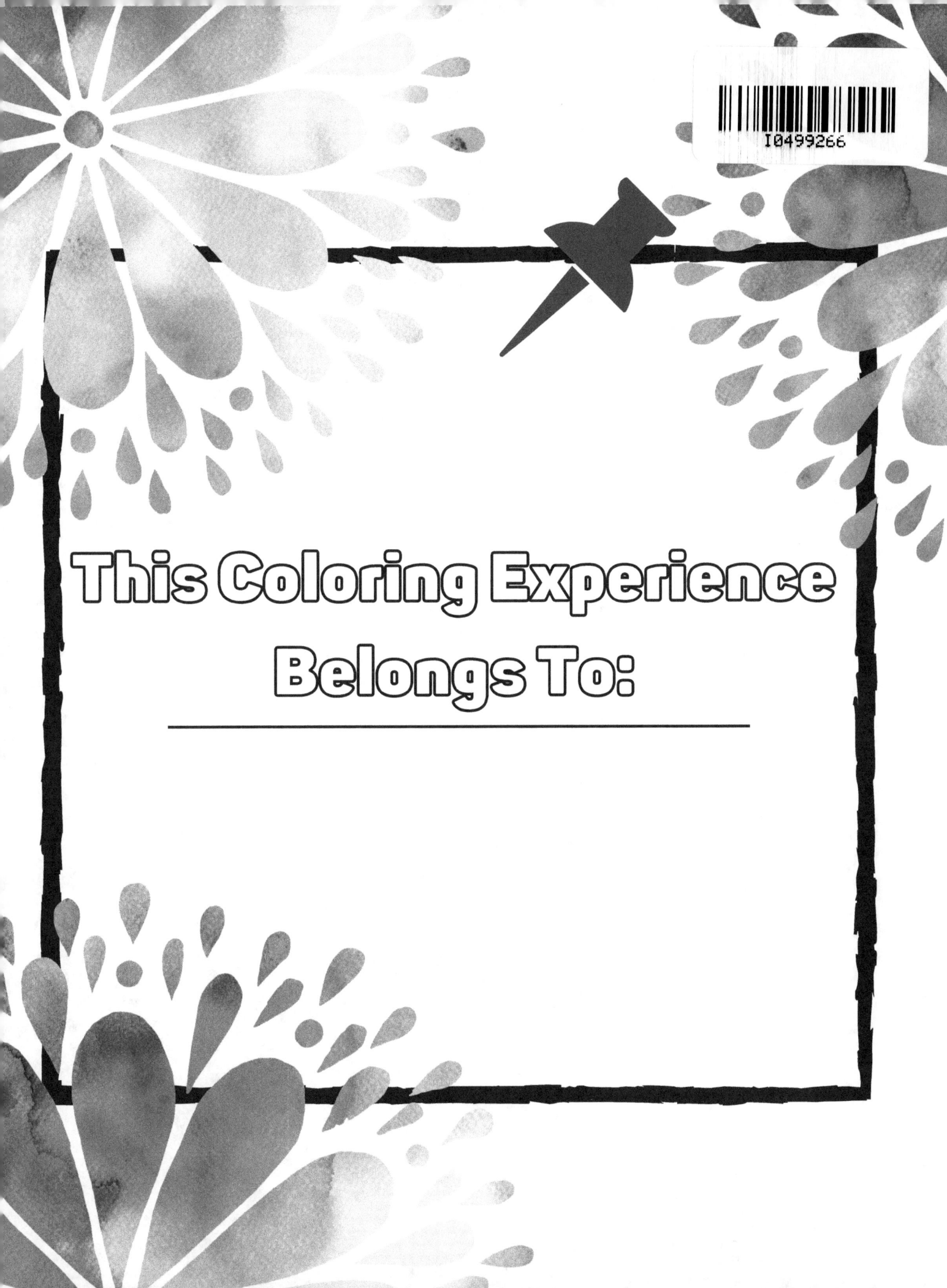

# Blu Impressions Designs, LLC

Website: shopbluimpressions.com
Email: info@bluimpressionsgraphics.com

ISBN: 978-1-6780-3150-3
Publisher: lulu.com

**Copyright © Blu Impressions Designs, LLC, 2022**
**All Rights Reserved.**

No part of this publication may be reproduced in any material form including photocopying of any pages without the written permission of the copyright owner.

Any illustrated pages may be photocopied for personal use but may not be reproduced for any other purposes without the written consent of Lena Payton Webb of Blu Impressions Designs, LLC.

# WELCOME

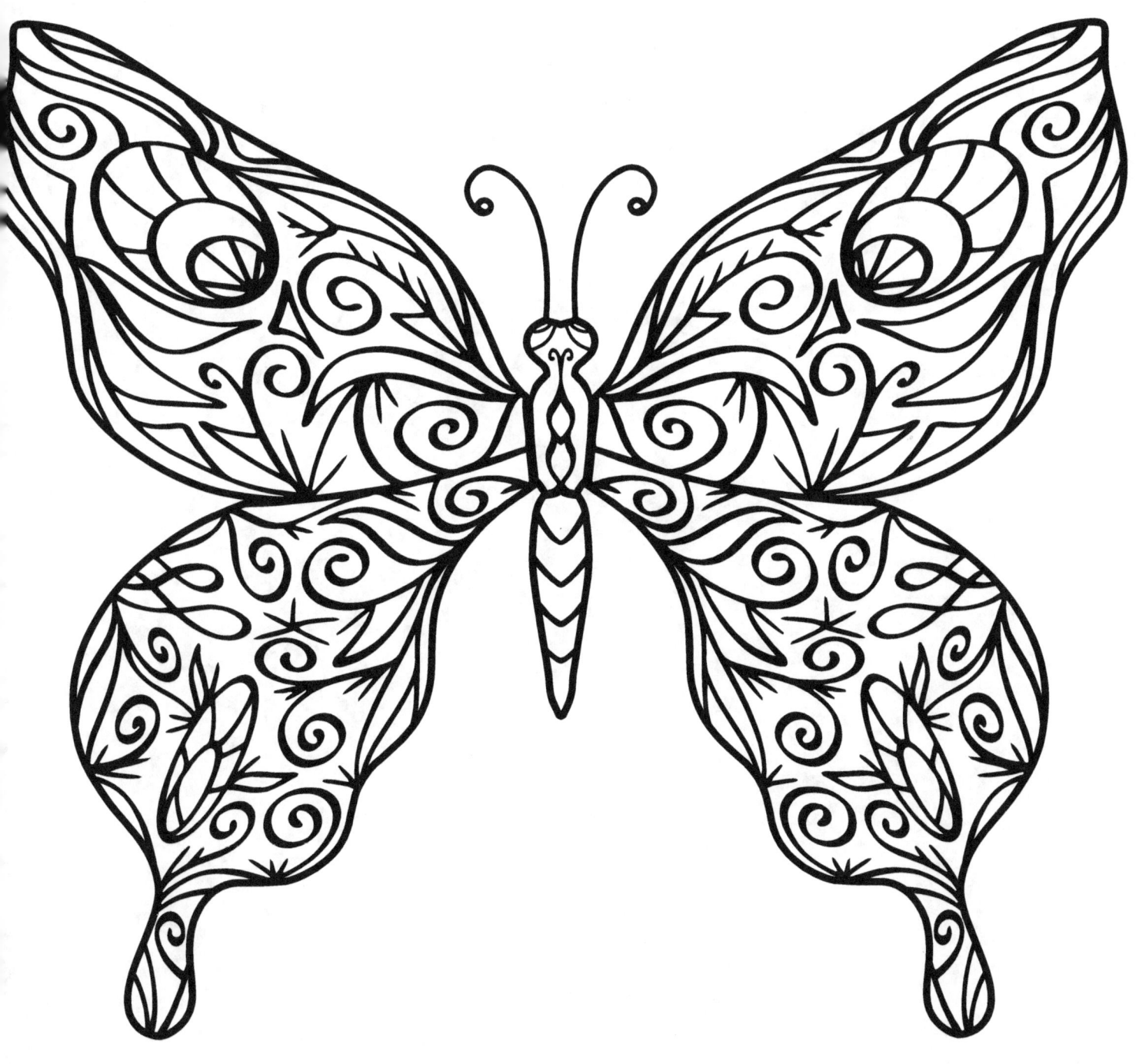

# MY PEACE
# MY PEACE
# MY PEACE
# MY PEACE

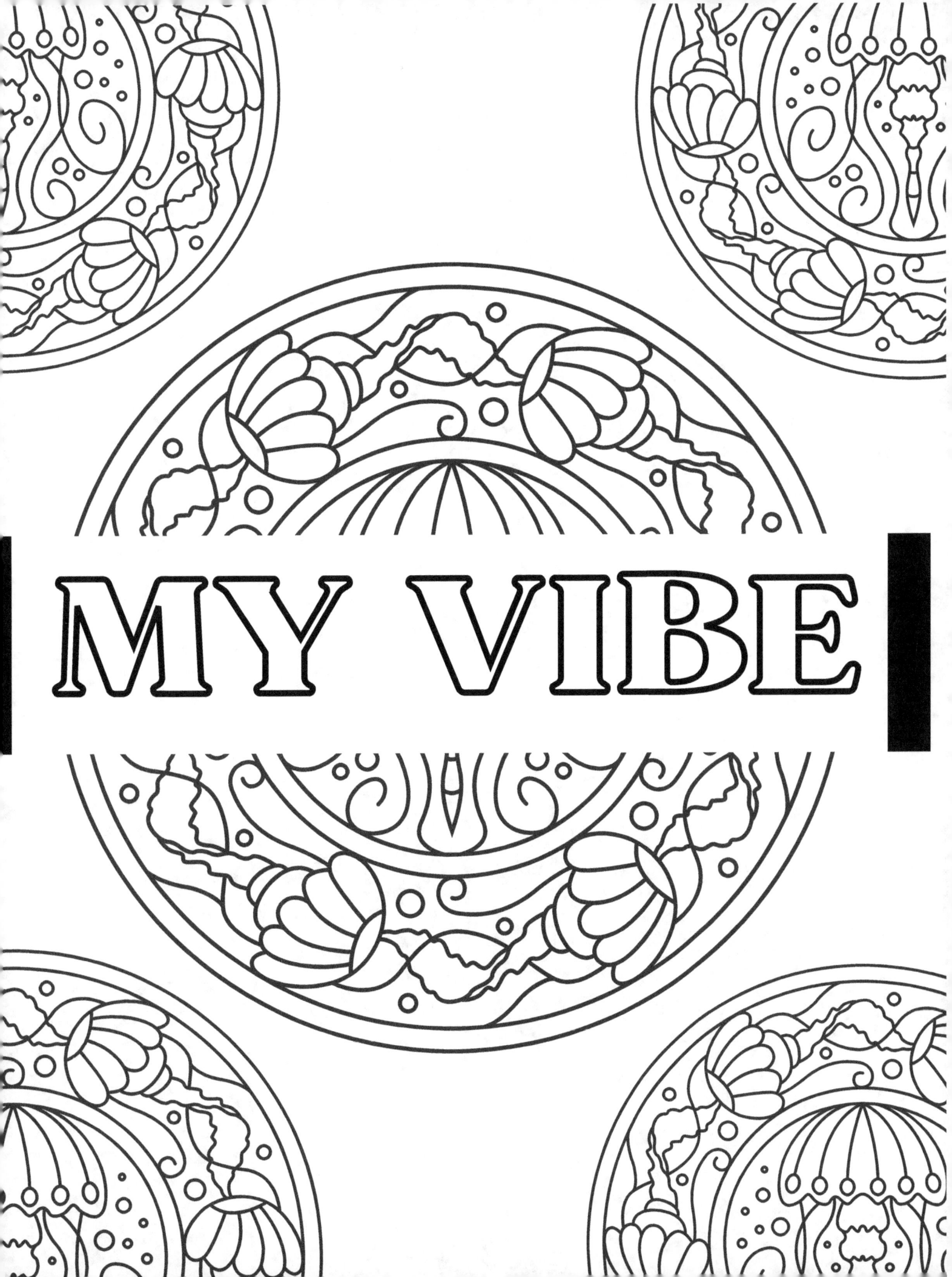

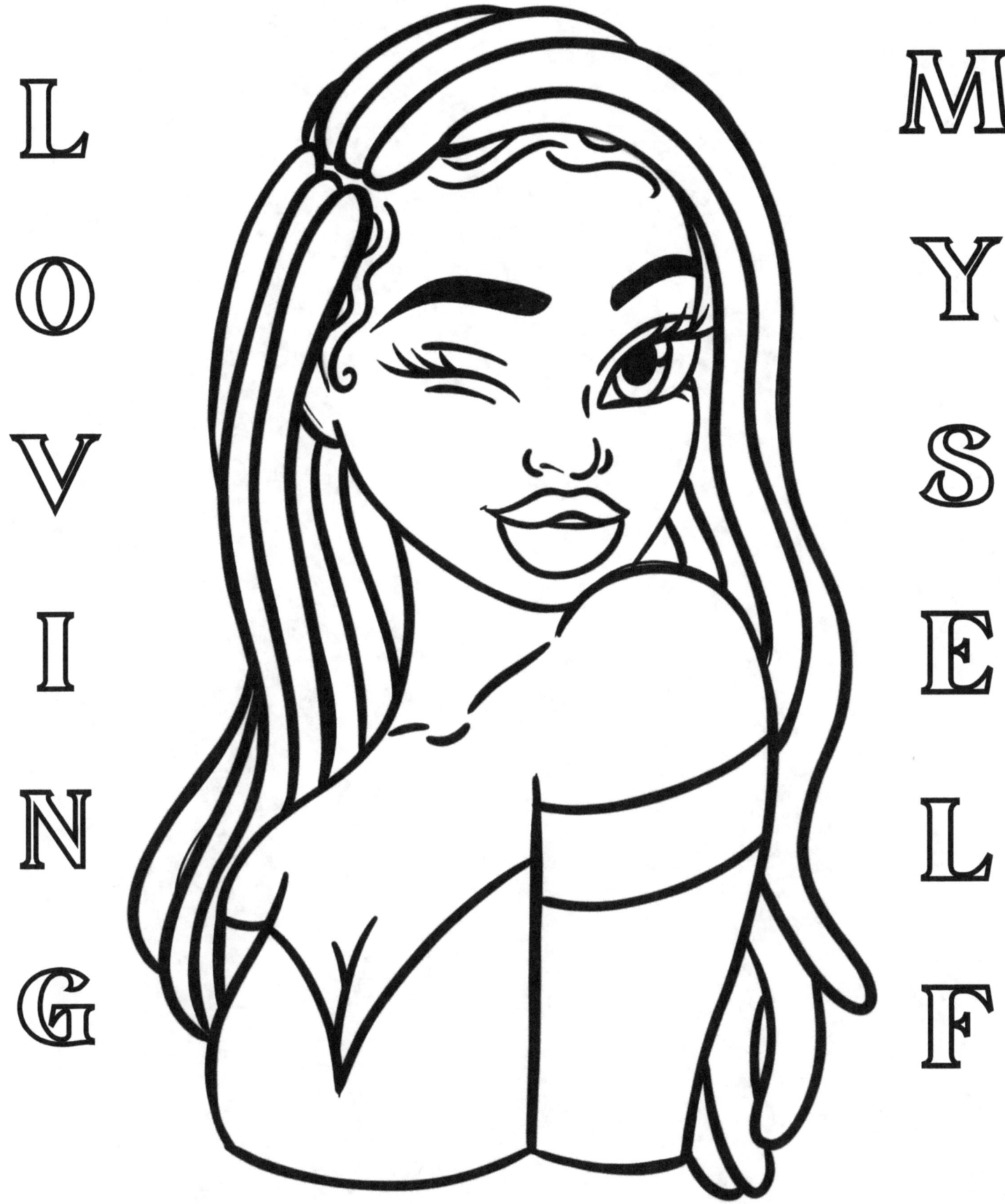

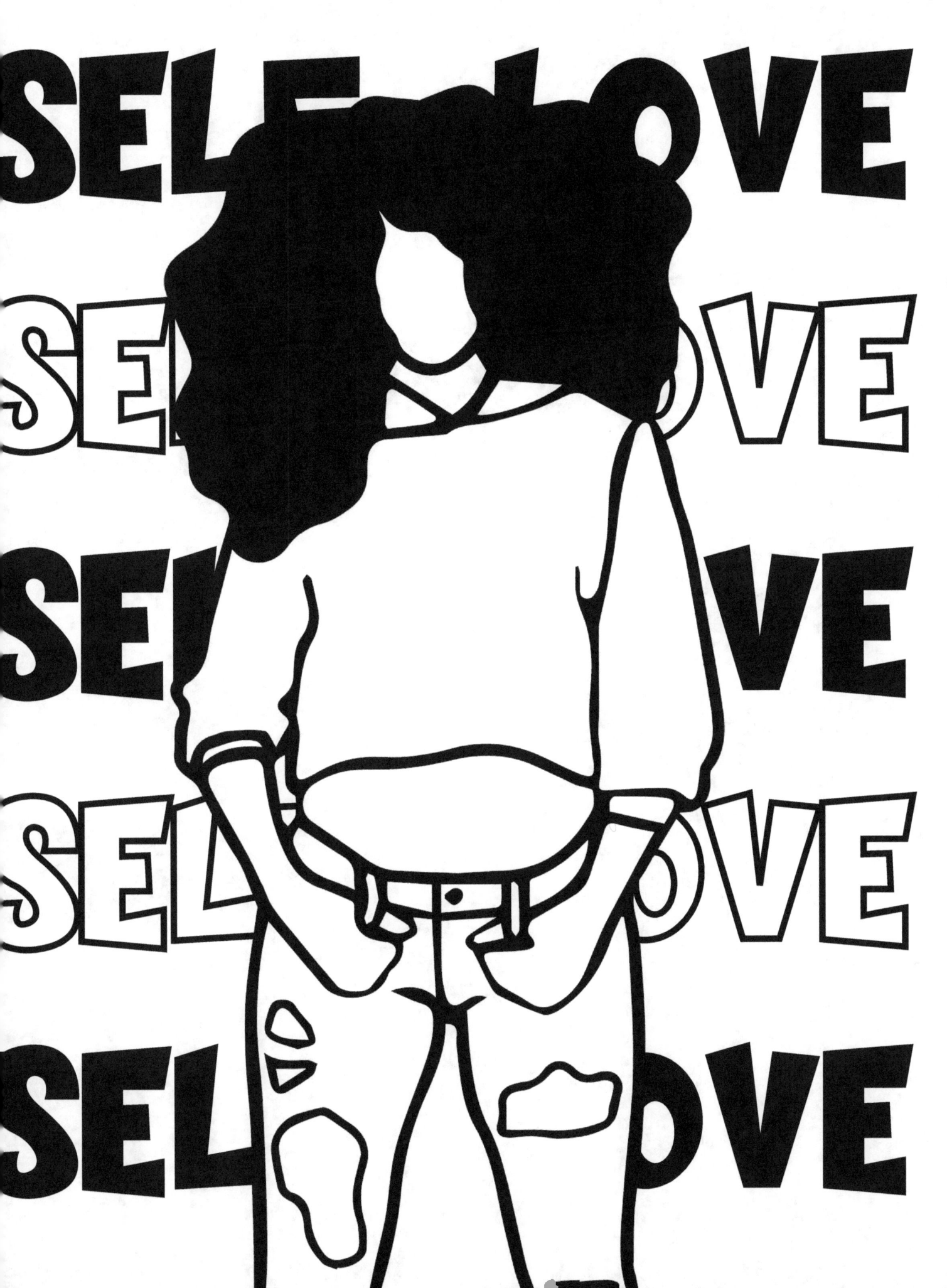

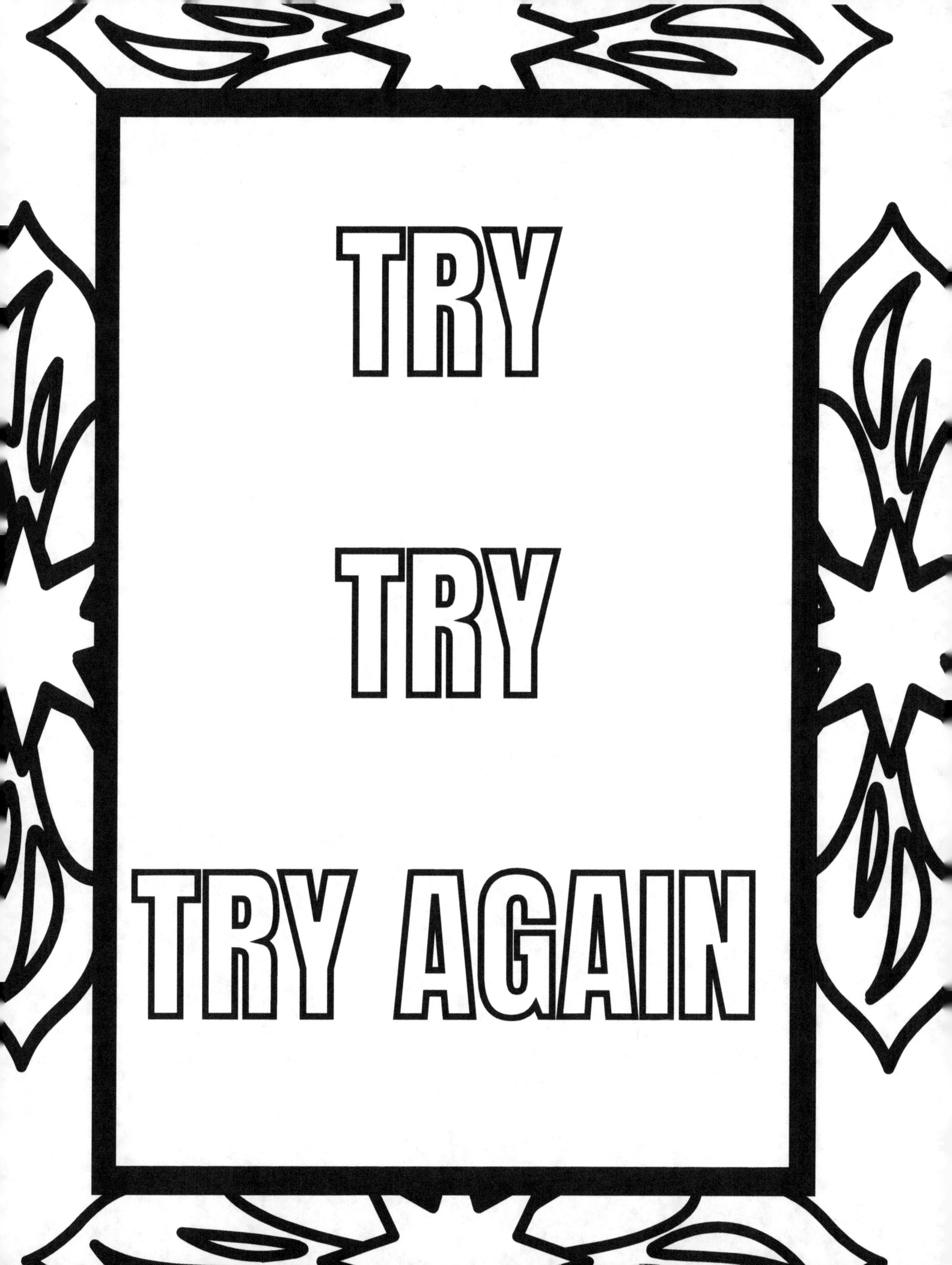

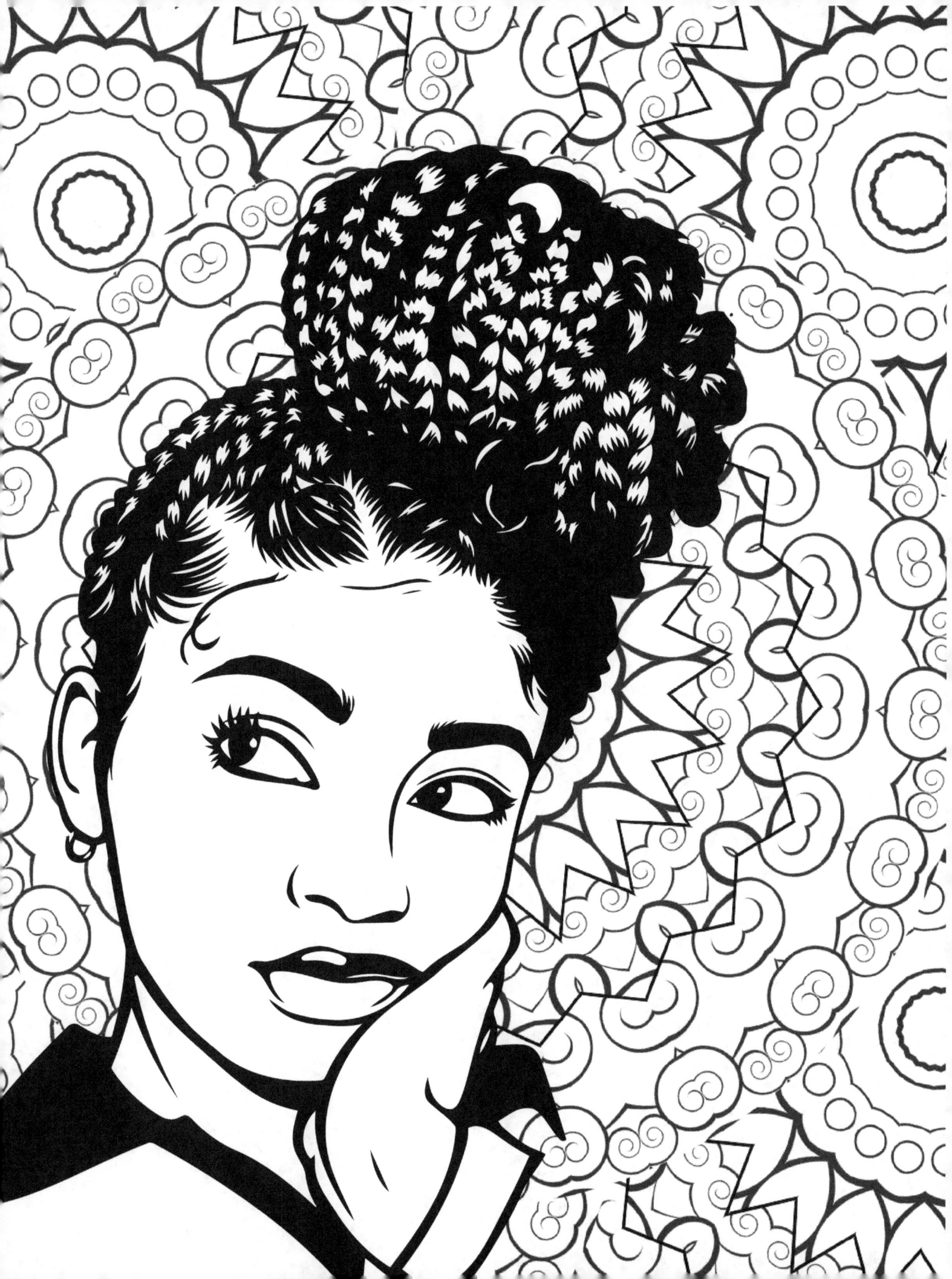

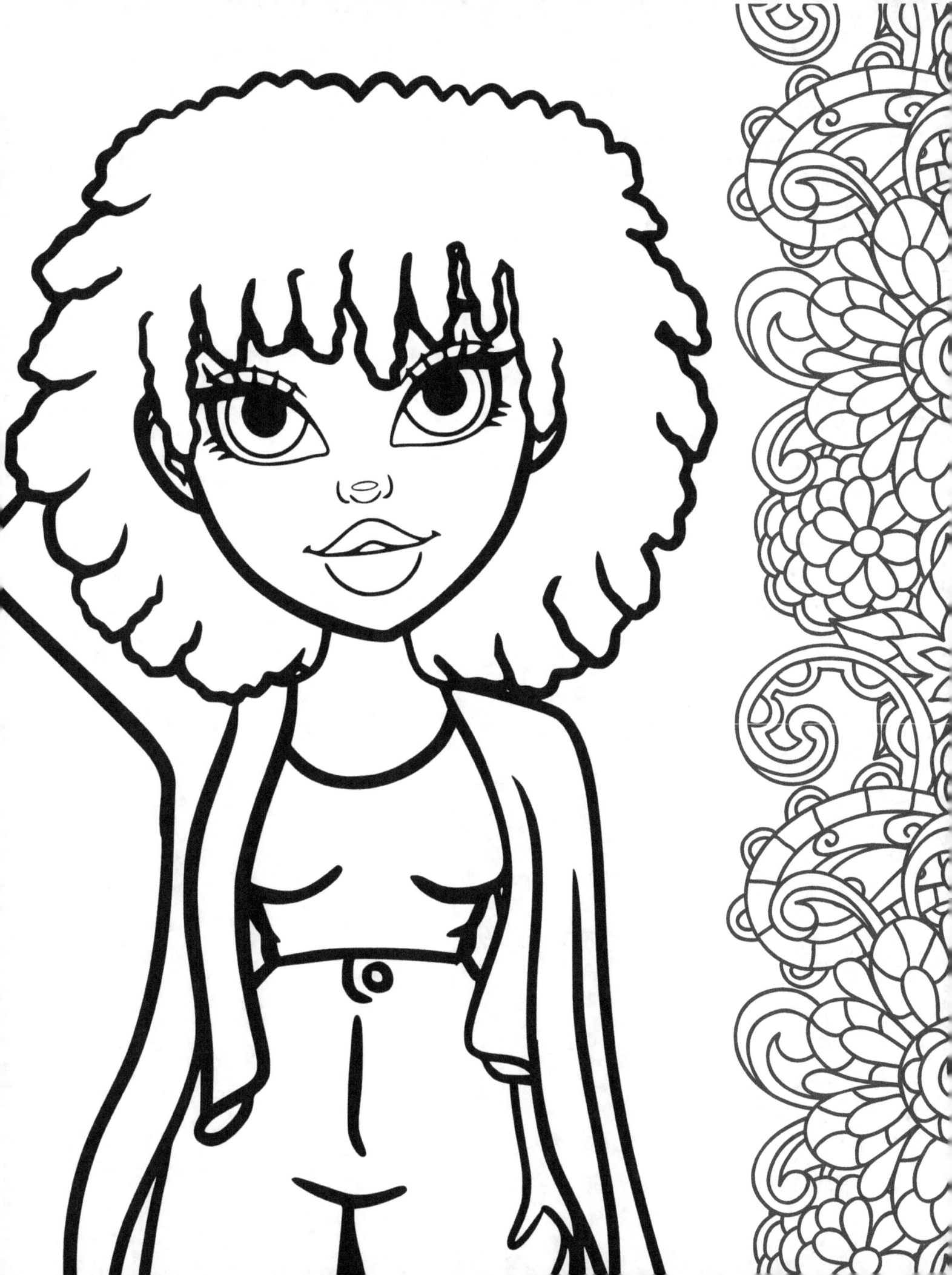

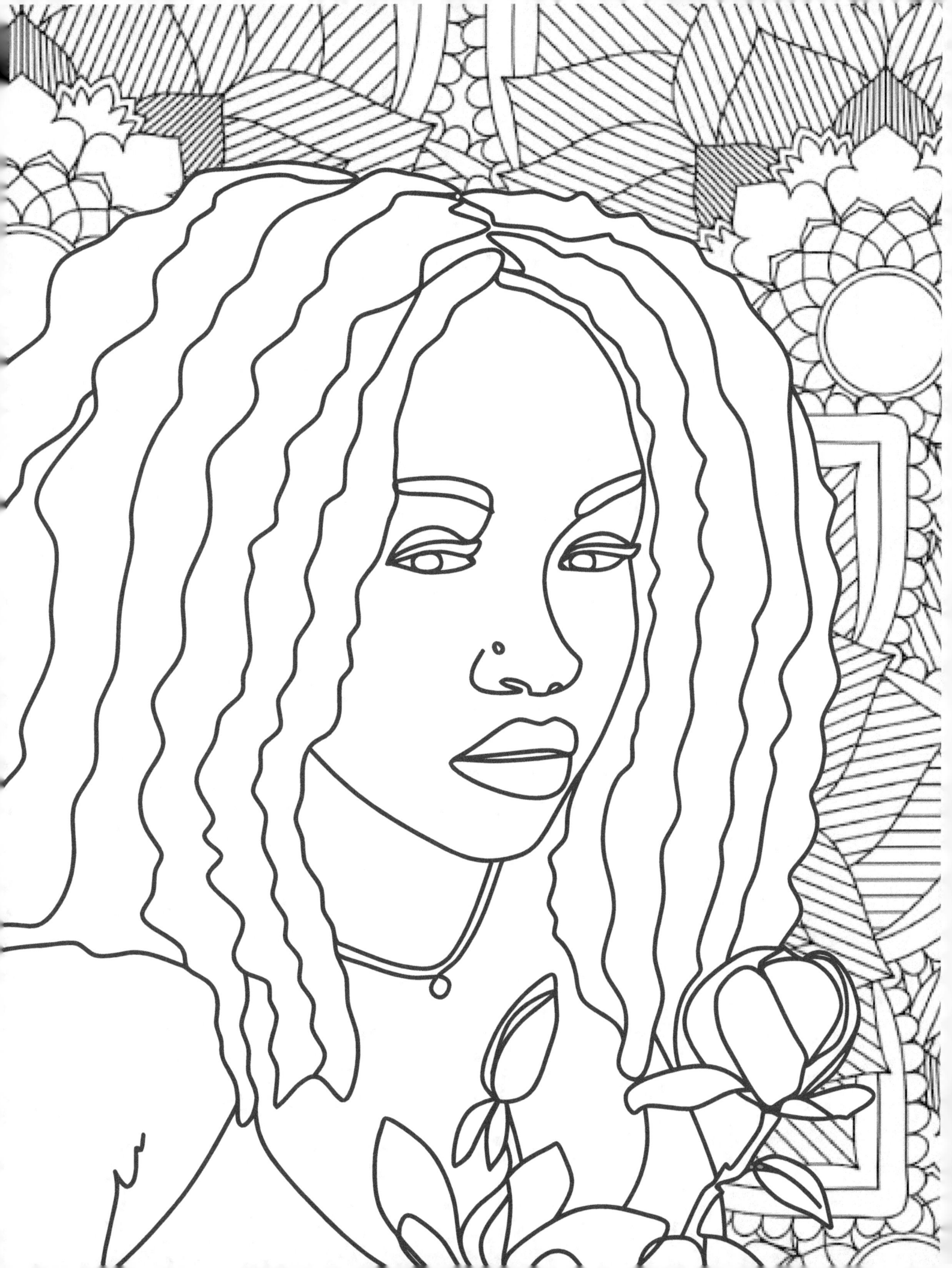

UNBOTHERED

UNBOTHERED

UNBOTHERED

UNBOTHERED

UNBOTHERED

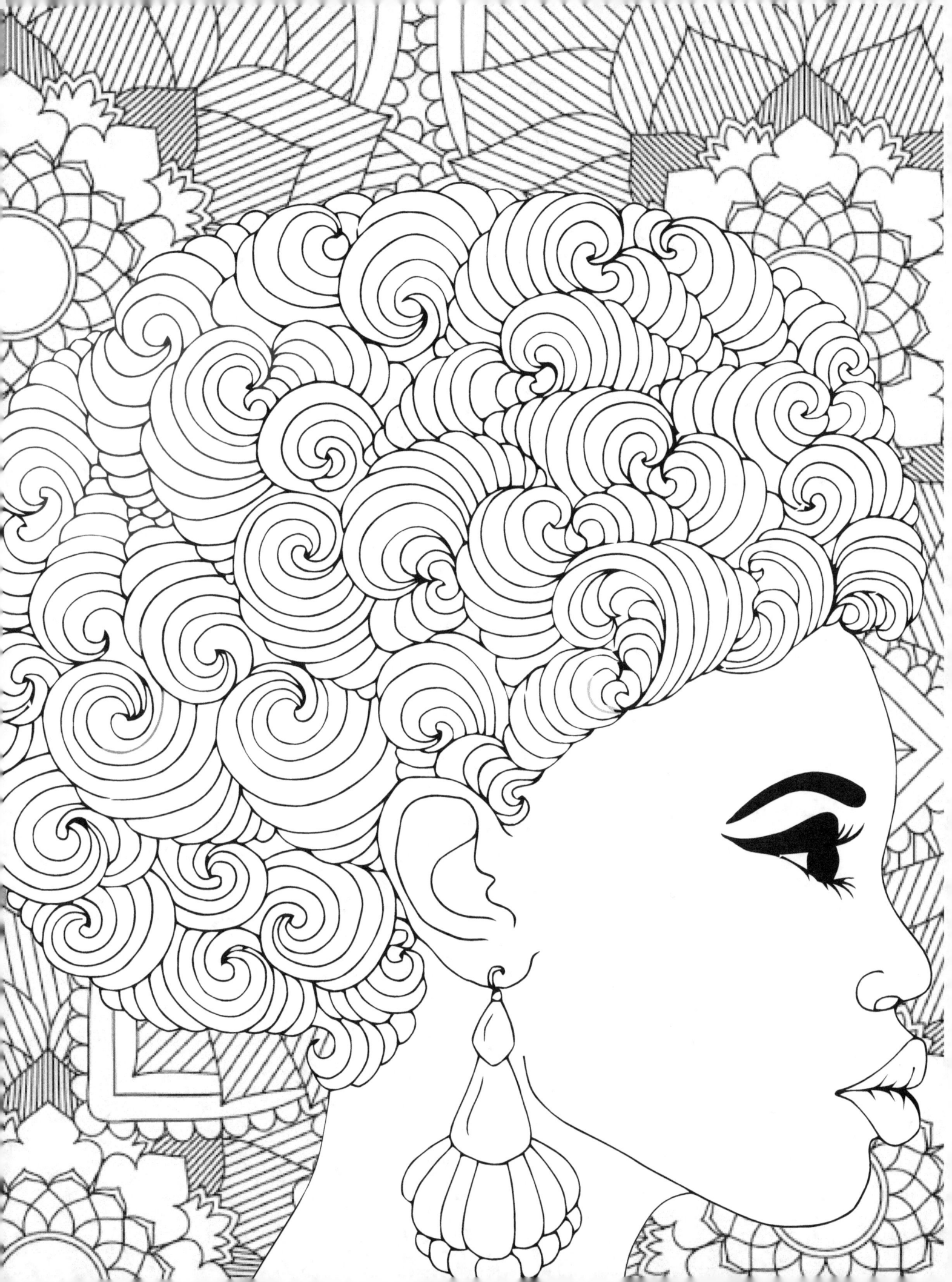

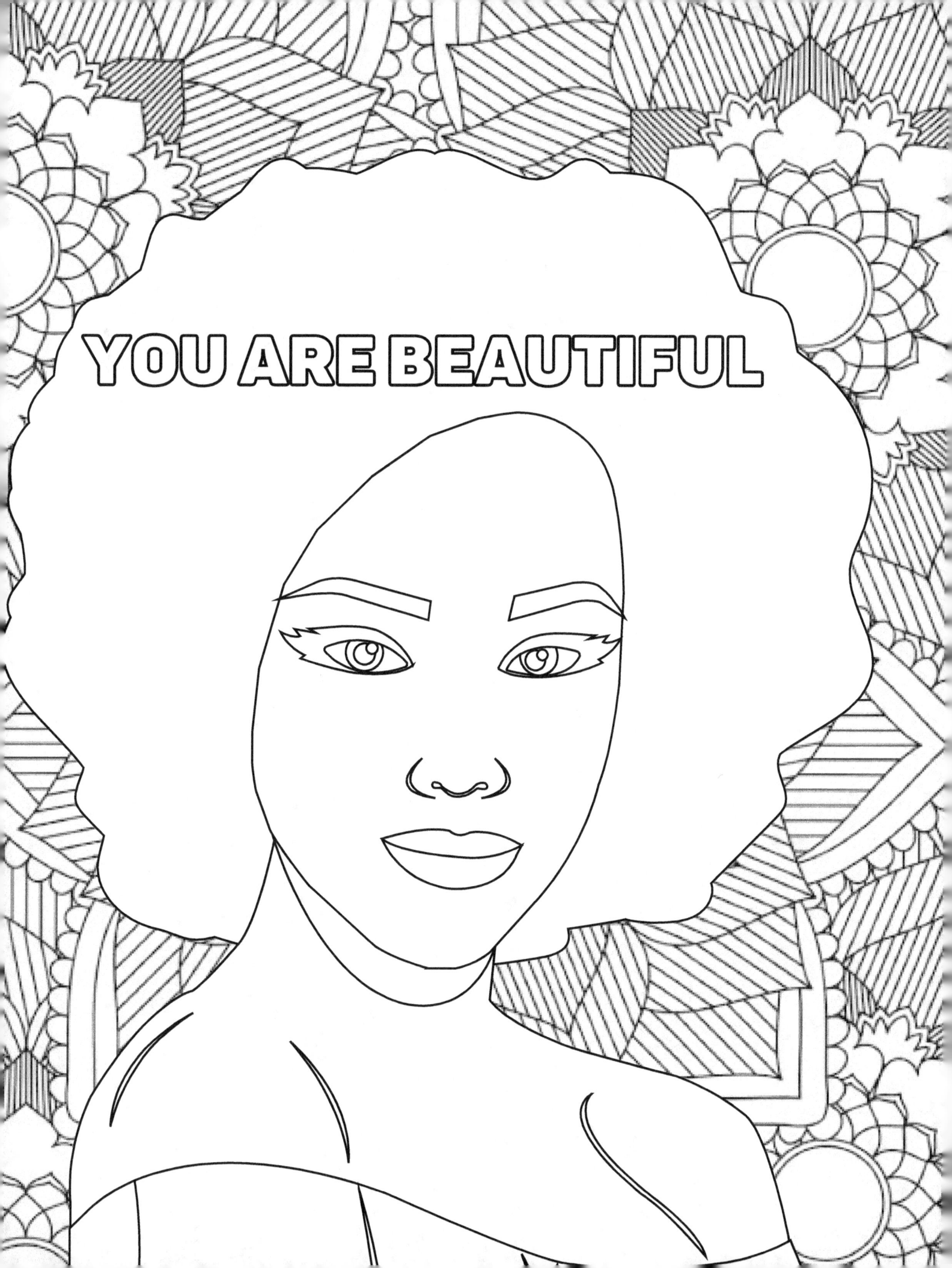

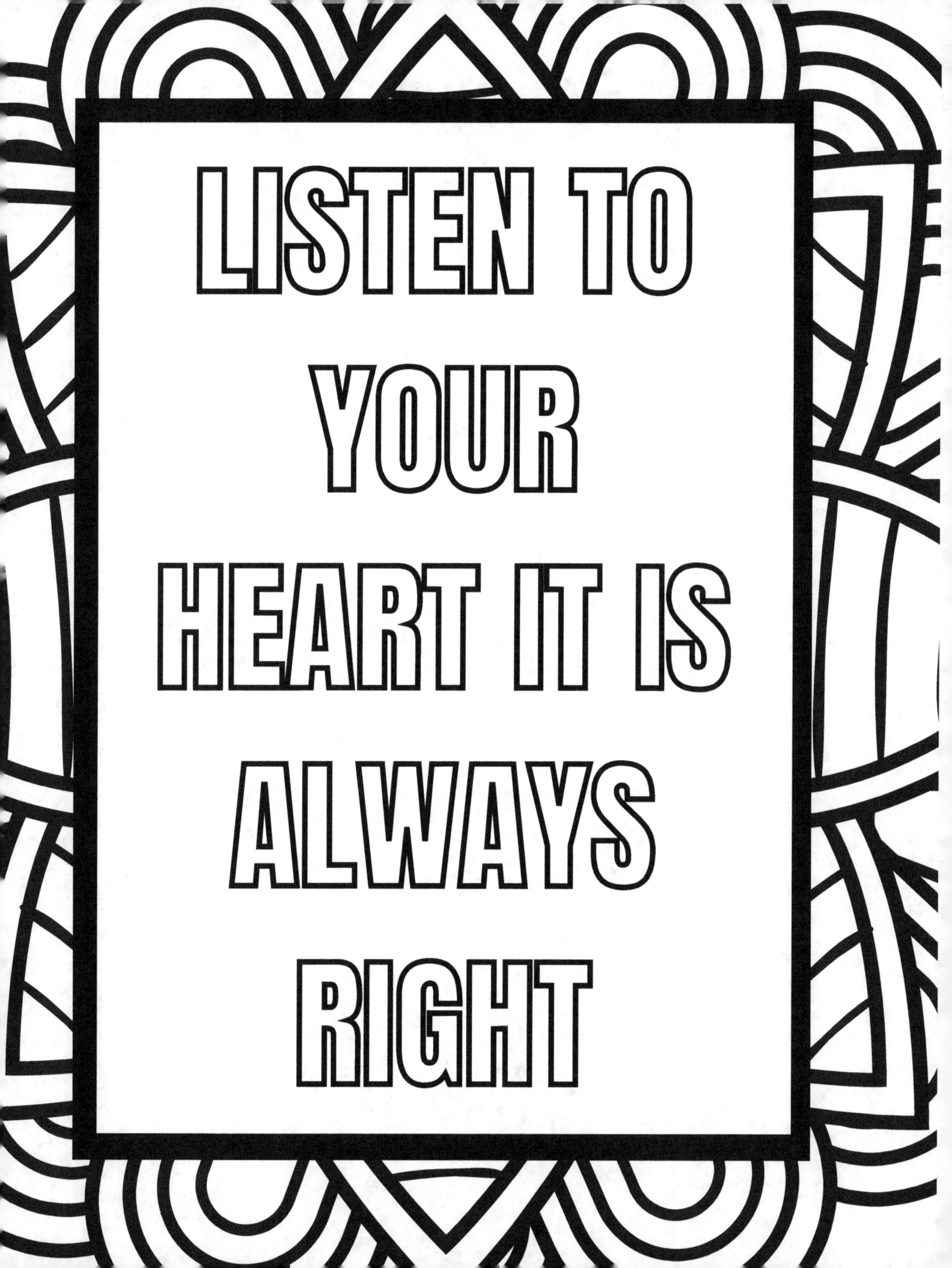

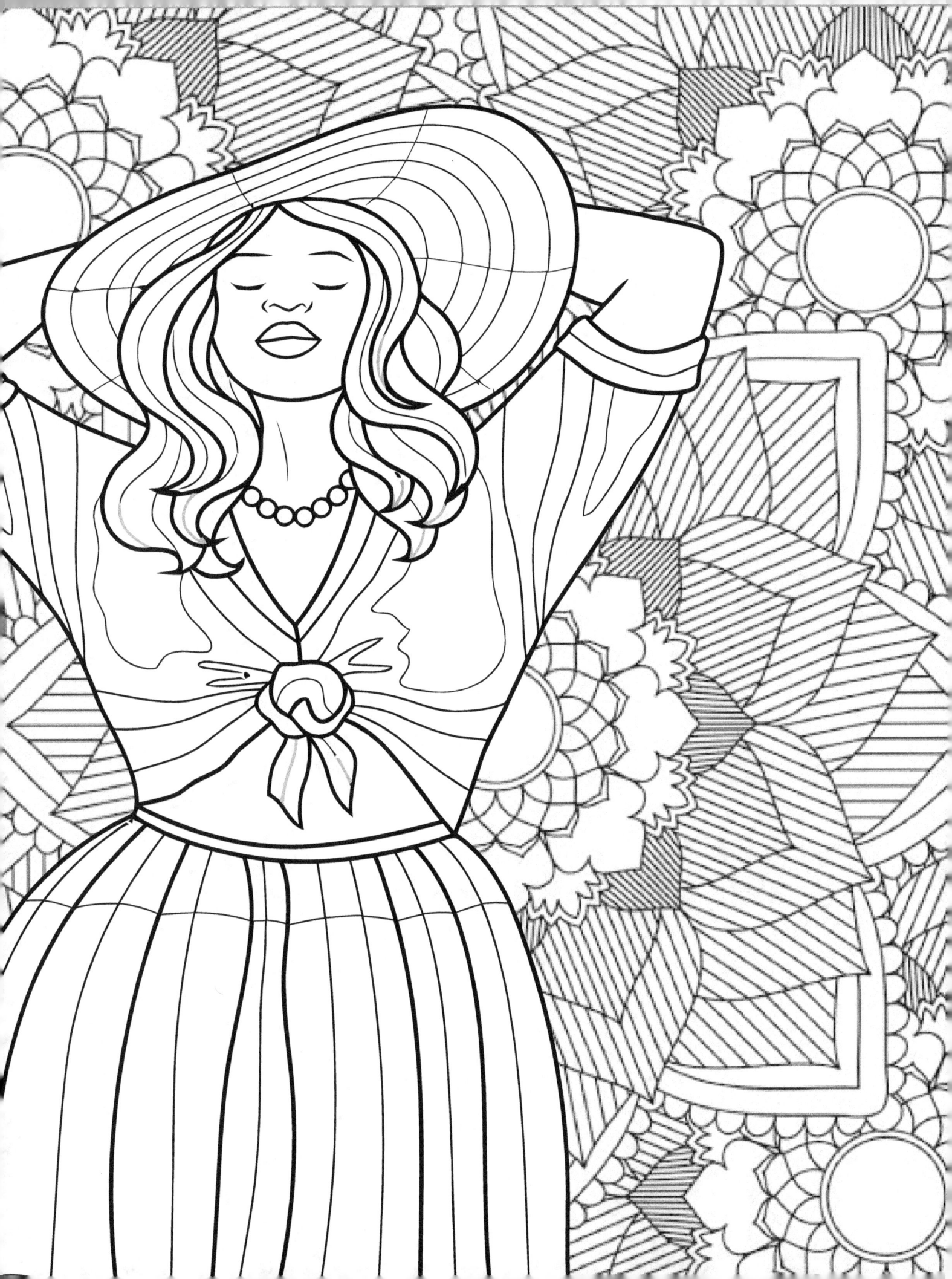

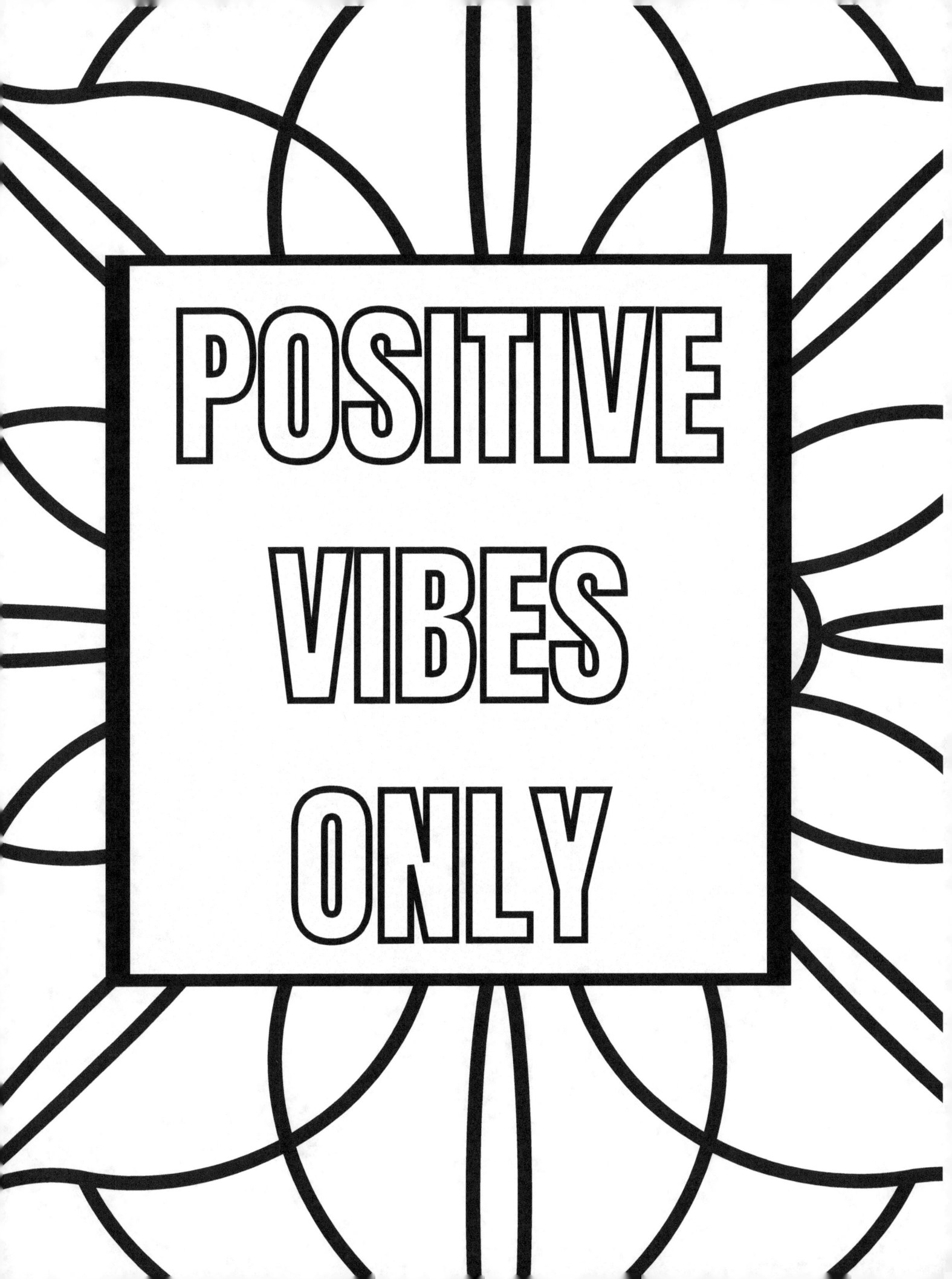

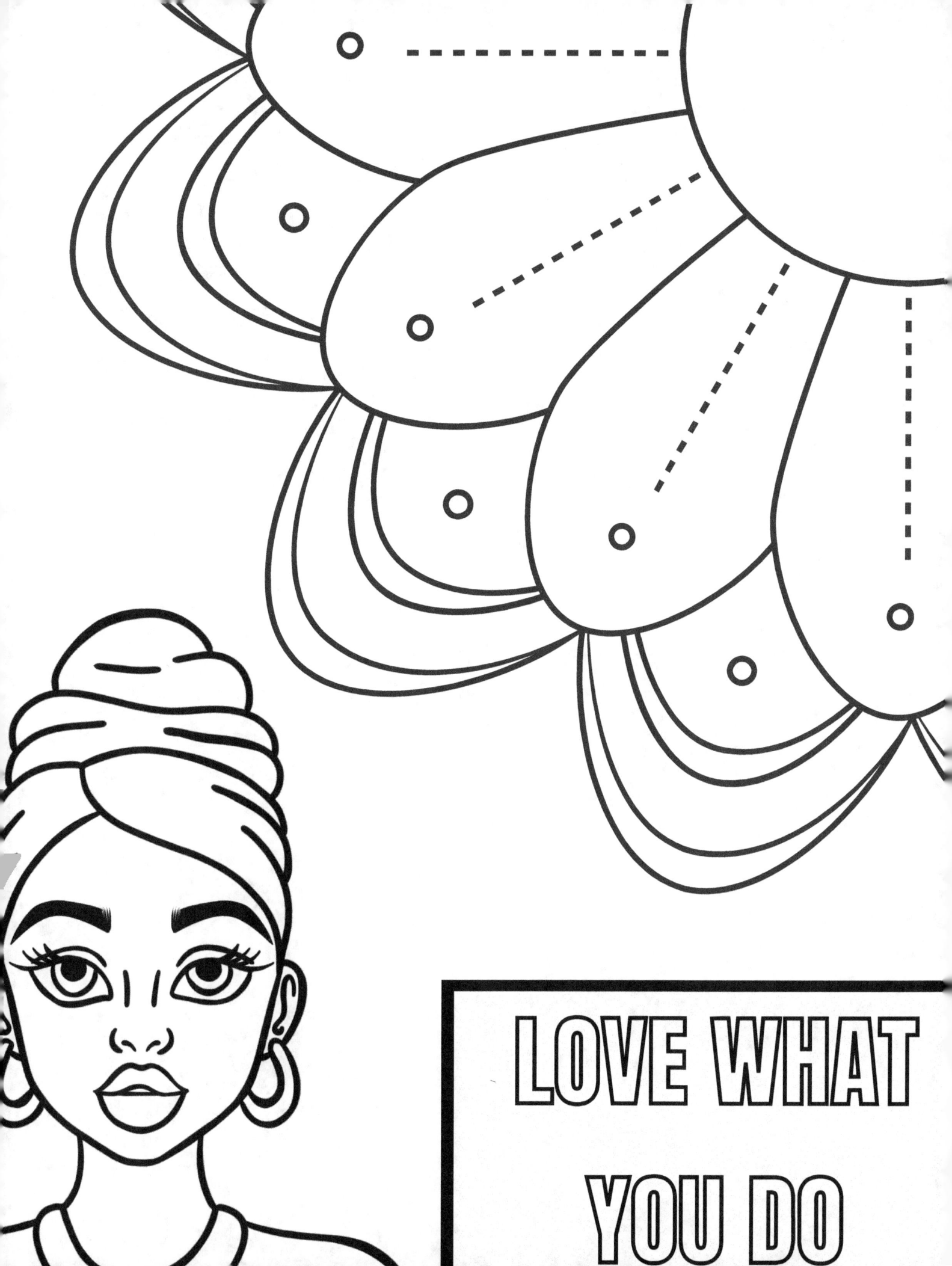

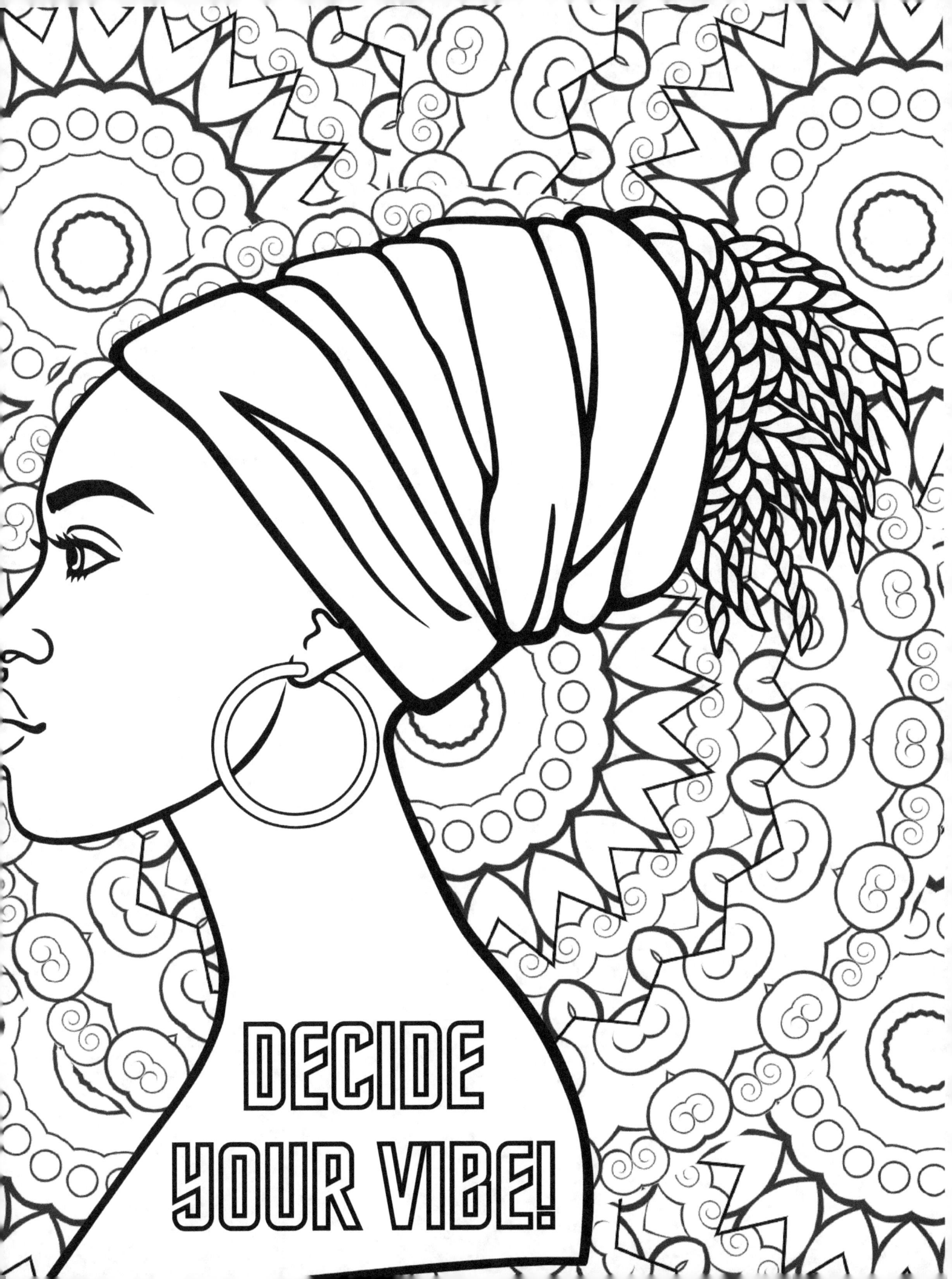